MW00450562

Overview of the Sarbanes-Oxley Act of 2002 with Other Changes in Auditing and the Public Accounting Profession

Integrated with:

*Auditing and Assurance Services:
An Integrated Approach,* 9th Edition

and

*Essentials of Auditing
and Assurance Services*

Overview of the Sarbanes-Oxley Act of 2002 with Other Changes in Auditing and the Public Accounting Profession

Integrated with:

*Auditing and Assurance Services:
An Integrated Approach,* 9th Edition

and

*Essentials of Auditing
and Assurance Services*

Alvin A. Arens • Randal J. Elder • Mark S. Beasley

PEARSON
Prentice
Hall

Upper Saddle River, New Jersey 07458

Editor-in-Chief: PJ Boardman
Acquisitions Editor: Bill Larkin
Assistant Editor: Sam Goffinet
Manager, Print Production: Christy Mahon
Production Editor & Buyer: Wanda Rockwell
Printer/Binder: VonHoffman Graphics, Inc., MD

Copyright © 2004 by Pearson Education, Inc., Upper Saddle River, New Jersey, 07458.
Pearson Prentice Hall. All rights reserved. Printed in the United States of America. This publication is protected by Copyright and permission should be obtained from the publisher prior to any prohibited reproduction, storage in a retrieval system, or transmission in any form or by any means, electronic, mechanical, photocopying, recording, or likewise. For information regarding permission(s), write to: Rights and Permissions Department.

Pearson Prentice Hall™ is a trademark of Pearson Education, Inc.

10 9 8 7 6 5 4 3 2 1
ISBN 0-13-144755-6

CONTENTS

Overview of the Sarbanes-Oxley Act of 2002 and Other Changes in Auditing and the Public Accounting Profession

Integrated with:

Auditing and Assurance Services: An Integrated Approach
9th Edition

&

Essentials of Auditing and Assurance Services [*]

Alvin A. Arens   Randal J. Elder   Mark S. Beasley

Pearson Prentice Hall, Inc.

[*] For *Essentials of Auditing and Assurance Services* users, please see chapter references at www.prenhall.com/arens.

INTRODUCTION

The Sarbanes-Oxley Act was signed into legislation on July 30, 2002. The provisions of the Act apply to publicly held companies and their audit firms, and will dramatically affect the accounting profession. The Act was triggered by the December 2001 bankruptcy of Enron less than a month after management admitted accounting errors that inflated earnings by almost $600 million since 1994. With $62 billion in assets, it was the largest bankruptcy case in U.S. history. However, it was dwarfed several months later by the massive fraud and bankruptcy filing of WorldCom in July 2002, with $100 billion in assets.

Enron and WorldCom were both audited by Arthur Andersen, a Big 5 audit firm. At one time the largest of the Big 5 firms, Andersen essentially ceased to exist after the firm was found guilty of obstruction of justice in the Enron case in June 2002. Reported instances of fraud and alleged audit failure at several other high-profile companies suggest that concerns about auditor performance were not limited to Andersen. Earlier concerns about auditor performance were expressed in 2000 by the Panel on Audit Effectiveness.

An important issue in the Enron case was the large amount of fees paid to Andersen for non-audit services. The SEC issued revised rules on auditor independence in 2000, including additional restrictions on the performance of non-audit services, due to independence concerns. The SEC had initially proposed prohibiting audit firms from providing any non-audit services to audit clients. Interestingly, Andersen was at one time the largest of the Big 5 accounting firms due to the size of its consulting practice. Andersen Consulting was the first consulting practice to separate from a Big 5 accounting firm, and three of the remaining Big 4 firms have since disposed of their consulting practices.

A key provision of the Sarbanes-Oxley Act is the creation of the Public Company Accounting Oversight Board (the PCAOB). The PCAOB will provide oversight for auditors of public companies, including establishing auditing and quality control standards for public company audits, and performing inspections of the quality controls at audit firms under its oversight. In addition, auditors must attest to management reports on the effectiveness of internal controls. Several other provisions of the Sarbanes-Oxley Act also had significant impacts on the accounting profession. A summary of the key provisions of the Act affecting public company audit firms is included in the Appendix.

Changes in fraud guidance and changes in the CPA exam are two additional changes that significantly affect the accounting profession. SAS No. 99 was issued in 2002 to provide additional guidance to auditors in identifying and responding to the risk of fraud. Cases of fraud at companies like Enron and WorldCom illustrate the range of fraud and the need for additional guidance for auditors in detecting fraud.

In April 2004, the paper-and-pencil CPA exam will change to a computer-based format. More importantly, the exam content will change to include simulations, as well as technology and other higher-order thinking skills now required of CPAs.

Significant provisions of the Sarbanes-Oxley Act and related changes in the accounting profession are described in the following pages. This is followed by discussion of the fraud guidance in SAS No. 99, along with an overview of proposed changes to the auditor's risk assessment process, and information on changes in the form and content of the Uniform CPA Examination.

CHANGES IN THE CPA PROFESSION

The demise of Andersen following the firm's indictment for obstruction of justice in the Enron case, and the disposition of their consulting practices by three of the remaining Big 4 firms, have dramatically changed the accounting profession.

Services Offered by Public Accounting Firms

The figure below illustrates the relationship among the services offered by CPA firms. The terms in the figure are described in Chapter 1 of *Auditing and Assurance Services: An Integrated Approach, 9th Edition*. Over the past 20 years, consulting services increased in importance and eventually became the largest source of revenue for most of the largest firms. The disposition of consulting practices and restrictions on consulting services due to SEC regulations and the Sarbanes-Oxley Act have significantly reduced the importance of management consulting services to CPA firm practices.

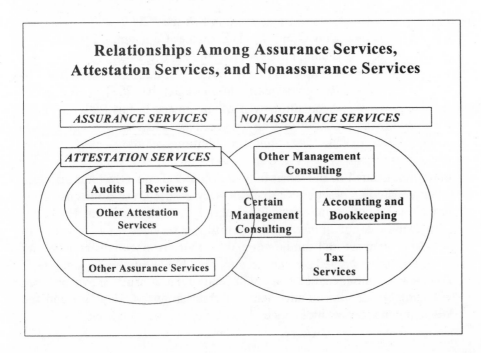

Relationships Among Assurance Services, Attestation Services, and Nonassurance Services

It is important to emphasize that CPA firms continue to provide consulting and other business advisory services. However, the ability to offer these services to publicly held audit clients is significantly reduced. Tax services continue to be a significant source of revenue, but certain tax services are likely to be restricted for audit clients due to concerns that these services might impair auditor independence.

Dispositions and Other Changes in Major Firm Consulting Practices

Three of the Big 4 accounting firms, as well as the former Andersen firm, have sold or otherwise disposed of their consulting practices. These changes were partially due to independence concerns and restrictions placed on consulting practices. These changes originated well before passage of the Sarbanes-Oxley Act, and even before the SEC issued its revisions to auditor independence rules in November 2000. The following table summarizes the changes involving the consulting practices of the major international accounting firms.

Changes in Consulting Practices of Major Accounting Firms

Former Consulting Practice Name	Changes in Firm Name and Ownership
Andersen Consulting	• Separated from Andersen in August 2000 • Renamed Accenture in January 2001 • Became a public company in July 2001
Deloitte Consulting	• Announced plans to separate as a private partnership and change name to Braxton in 2002 • Terminated plans to separate from Deloitte & Touche in March 2003
Ernst & Young Consulting	• Sold to CapGemini in February 2000 • Consulting firm is known as CapGemini Ernst & Young but is not part of Ernst & Young
KPMG Consulting	• Completed initial public offering in February 2001 • Renamed BearingPoint in October 2002
PricewaterhouseCoopers Consulting	• Acquisition by IBM announced in July 2002

As illustrated in the table, only Deloitte & Touche has not disposed of its consulting practice. Sarbanes-Oxley restricts the ability of CPA firms to offer consulting services to publicly held audit clients. However, CPA firms are not limited in the consulting services they can offer to private companies and public companies that are not audit clients, and can offer non-restricted services to publicly held audit clients. Deloitte & Touche has announced that they will retain their consulting practice, but still comply with the requirements of the Sarbanes-Oxley Act and the SEC's independence rules.

The first part of the table on the following page presents the ranking of the Big 4 accounting firms based on fiscal year 2002 revenue, along with information on the number of partners, professionals, U.S. offices, and mix of practice revenues. The second part of the table presents comparative data based on fiscal year 2000 information.

Because it has not disposed of its consulting practice, Deloitte & Touche is now the largest accounting firm, and derives more of its revenue from consulting than the other Big 4 firms. The comparative data indicate that the remaining Big 4 firms are smaller, and derive a much larger percentage of revenues from audit and other attest services, and a much smaller percentage of revenues from consulting services. The fiscal year 2000 data indicates that Andersen was the fifth largest CPA firm. Prior to the separation of Andersen Consulting (now Accenture) in 2000, Andersen was the largest accounting firm, and derived 66 percent of its revenues from consulting.

CHANGES IN THE REGULATORY ENVIRONMENT

Sarbanes-Oxley dramatically changes oversight of the profession by establishing the Public Company Accounting Oversight Board, which has been appointed and will be overseen by the SEC. The Board is made up of five full-time members and will oversee and investigate the audits and auditors of public companies. As required by Sarbanes-Oxley, the SEC announced on April 24, 2003 that the PCAOB was appropriately organized and able to carry out the requirements of the Sarbanes-Oxley Act.

Establishment of Public Company Accounting Oversight Board (PCAOB)

- *Board composition* - Two of the five Board members must be or must have been CPAs. The remaining three must not be and cannot have been CPAs. The Chair may be held by one of the CPA members, but must not have practiced accounting during the five years preceding his or her appointment.
- *Funding* – The PCAOB will be funded by mandatory fees on public companies. Accounting firms that audit public companies must register with the PCAOB ("registered firm") and pay registration and annual fees.
- *Standard setting* – The Board will issue or adopt standards set by other groups for audit firm quality controls for the audits of public companies. These standards include auditing and related attestation standards, quality control, ethics, independence, and "other standards necessary to protect the public interest."
- *Investigative and disciplinary authority* – The Board can regularly inspect registered accounting firms' operations and will investigate potential violations of securities laws, professional standards, competency, and conduct.

5

Revenue and Other Data for the Largest CPA Firms in the United States

Fiscal Year 2002

Size by Revenue	Firm	Net Revenue – U.S. Only (in $ millions)	Partners	Professionals	U.S. Offices	Percentage of Total Revenue from Accounting and Auditing/Tax/Management Consulting/Other
1	Deloitte & Touche	$5,933.0	2,618	19,835	81	36/21/34/9
2	PricewaterhouseCoopers	$5,174.0	2,624	29,787	150	58/30/9/3
3	Ernst & Young	$4,515.0	2,118	15,078	86	59/38/0/3
4	KPMG	$3,400.0	1,500	11,000	132	44/36/20/0

Source: *Accounting Today:* March 17-April 6, 2003/www.webcpa.com

Fiscal Year 2000

Size by Revenue	Firm	Net Revenue – U.S. Only (in $ millions)	Partners	Professionals	U.S. Offices	Percentage of Total Revenue from Accounting and Auditing/Tax/Management Consulting
1	PricewaterhouseCoopers	$8,878.0	2,932	34,151	186	33/17/50
2	Deloitte & Touche	$5,838.0	2,155	20,658	103	31/19/50
3	KPMG	$5,400.0	1,500	19,000	145	35/22/43
4	Ernst & Young	$4,270.0	1,946	13,653	82	57/38/5
5	Andersen	$3,600.0	1,313	17,600	80	45/30/25

Source: *Accounting Today* ("The Electronic Accountant" - http://www.electronicaccountant.com/html/t100y2k/tocp3.htm)

Appointment of PCAOB Board Members – Appointment of a chairman of the PCAOB proved to be challenging. Former CIA and FBI chief William Webster was appointed chairman in October 2002 in a contested vote, but resigned three weeks later due to controversy involving his role as head of the audit committee of a company involved in questionable accounting. William McDonough, former head of the New York branch of the Federal Reserve, was subsequently appointed chairman in April 2003.

The Sarbanes-Oxley Act provides that the PCAOB shall establish auditing, quality control, and ethics standards to be followed by registered CPA firms in their audits of public companies. The Act allowed the PCAOB to designate or recognize a professional group of accountants to propose new standards. However, in April 2003 the PCAOB announced that they would not delegate this authority, and will assume responsibility for establishing standards.

Auditing Standards

The PCAOB has identified three priorities:

- A review of existing professional standards
- Consideration of auditing standards required by the Act
- A review of standards for an auditor's attestation of internal controls for public companies

Existing auditing standards remain in effect until the PCAOB has completed its review of standards. The Auditing Standards Board (ASB) of the AICPA has a number of current proposed standards related to audit risk, and the AICPA has urged the PCAOB to make consideration of these proposed standards a priority.

The AICPA continues to have responsibility for setting professional standards for nonpublic companies. It is possible that there will be different standards for the audit of public and nonpublic companies.

Similar to the requirements for auditing standards, Sarbanes-Oxley specified criteria for accounting principles to be recognized as "generally accepted" by the SEC. In April 2003 the SEC announced that it will continue to recognize statements issued by the Financial Accounting Standards Board as being generally accepted.

Accounting Standards

The PCAOB also has responsibility for establishing quality control standards for auditors of public companies. The SEC declared the PCAOB operational on April 25, 2003. Accounting firms that "prepare or issue" or "participate" in the preparation of an audit report for an "issuer" must register with the PCAOB within 180 days of that date. An issuer is

Quality Control

defined in the Sarbanes-Oxley Act, and includes public companies subject to SEC regulation under the Securities and Exchange Act of 1934 and issuers of securities under the Securities Act of 1933.

The PCAOB will conduct inspections of each registered accounting firm to assess the firm's compliance with the rules of the PCAOB and SEC, professional standards, and the firm's own quality control policies. Any violations could result in disciplinary action by the Board and be reported to the SEC and state accountancy boards. Annual inspections are required for accounting firms that audit more than 100 issuers, and at least once every three years for other registered firms.

The Public Oversight Board (POB) had been responsible for oversight of public company audits through its oversight of peer review and other regulatory programs of the SEC Practice Section of the AICPA. The POB voted to disband effective May 1, 2002 in response to plans by the SEC to reorganize the regulatory structure of public company audits following the Enron collapse and other perceived audit failures.

Reports on Public Company Internal Control

Some public companies had already voluntarily issued reports on internal control, and such reports have been required in certain industries, such as banking. Now the Sarbanes-Oxley Act requires all public companies to issue an "internal control report" which includes:

- A statement that management is responsible for establishing and maintaining an adequate internal control structure and procedures for financial reporting.
- An assessment of the effectiveness of the internal control structure and procedures for financial reporting as of the end of the company's fiscal year.

The company's auditor must attest to and issue a report on management's assessment of internal control. As previously noted, the PCAOB has made the review of standards related to attestation of internal control one of its first three priorities.

SEC requirements – In May 2003, the SEC adopted rules dealing with the certification of internal control. Under the final rules, in addition to a statement that management is responsible for establishing and maintaining internal control, the report must contain a statement identifying the framework used by management to evaluate the effectiveness of internal control. Management must also disclose any material weaknesses in internal control and will be unable to conclude that the company's internal control over financial reporting is effective if there are one or more material weaknesses.

Management's evaluation must be based on a recognized control framework that has been established by a body or group that followed a due-process procedure that allows for public comment. The internal control framework for most U.S. companies will be the Committee of

Sponsoring Organizations (COSO) *Internal Control – Integrated Framework*.

The SEC rules define internal control over financial reporting as a process designed by or under the supervision of the company's chief executive and chief financial officers to provide reasonable assurance regarding the reliability of financial reporting and the preparation of financial statements for external purposes in accordance with generally accepted accounting principles and includes policies and procedures that:

- pertain to the maintenance of records that in reasonable detail accurately and fairly reflect the transactions and dispositions of the assets of the company;
- provide reasonable assurance that transactions are recorded to permit preparation of financial statements in accordance with generally accepted accounting principles, and receipts and expenditures are being made only in accordance with authorizations of management and the directors of company;
- provide reasonable assurance regarding prevention or timely detection of unauthorized acquisition, use or disposition of company assets that could have a material effect on the financial statements.

Companies with market capitalization over $75 million must comply with the reporting requirements for fiscal years ending on or after June 15, 2004. All other companies must comply for their fiscal years ending on or after April 15, 2005.

Auditing Standards Board Exposure Draft – The ASB has issued an exposure draft on attestation engagements related to reporting on internal control. As discussed previously, the PCAOB has announced that it will not delegate standard setting for public companies to the ASB. The exposure draft provides for combined or separate reporting on the company's financial statements and management's assertion about the effectiveness of internal control. The following page provides an example of a combined report based on the exposure draft.

Because the audit of the financial statements and management's assertion about internal control is an integrated activity, the date of the auditor's opinion on the financial statements and the auditor's opinion about internal control should be the same. Note that the report, in addition to referring to the report on management's assertion on internal control, includes an additional paragraph on inherent limitations of internal control. The audit opinion on the financial statements addresses

Sample Combined Report on Financial Statements and Internal Control

Independent Auditor's Report

Introductory Paragraph

We have audited the accompanying balance sheets of Westbrook Company, Inc. as of December 31, 2003 and 2002, and the related statements of income, stockholders' equity and comprehensive income, and cash flows for each of the years in the three-year period ended December 31, 2003. We have also audited management's assertion included in the accompanying management report on internal control that Westbrook Company, Inc. maintained effective internal control over financial reporting as of December 31, 2003, based on criteria established in *Internal Control-Integrated Framework* issued by the Committee of Sponsoring Organizations of the Treadway Commission (COSO). Management's assertion also states that effective internal control over financial reporting includes *(a)* maintenance of records that in reasonable detail accurately and fairly reflect the transactions and dispositions of the assets of the Company, and *(b)* policies and procedures that provide reasonable assurance that *(1)* transactions are recorded as necessary to permit preparation of financial statements in accordance with accounting principles generally accepted in the United States of America, and *(2)* receipts and expenditures of the Company are being made only in accordance with authorizations of management and directors of the Company. These financial statements and management's assertion about the effectiveness of internal control over financial reporting are the responsibility of the Company's management. Our responsibility is to express an opinion on these financial statements and management's assertion based on our audits.

Scope Paragraph

We conducted our audits in accordance with auditing standards generally accepted in the United States of America. Those standards require that we plan and perform the audits to obtain reasonable assurance about whether the financial statements and management's assertion are free of material misstatement. An audit of financial statements includes examining, on a test basis, evidence supporting the amounts and disclosures in the financial statements, assessing the accounting principles used and significant estimates made by management, and evaluating the overall financial statement presentation. An audit of internal control includes obtaining an understanding of internal control over financial reporting, testing and evaluating the design and overall effectiveness of internal control, and performing such other procedures as we considered necessary in the circumstances. We believe that our audits provide a reasonable basis for our opinions.

Inherent Limitations Paragraph

Because of the inherent limitations of internal control over financial reporting, including the possibility of management override of controls, misstatements due to error or fraud may occur and not be detected. Also, projection of any evaluation of internal control over financial reporting to future periods are subject to the risk that internal control may become inadequate because of changes in conditions, or that the degree of compliance with the policies or procedures may deteriorate.

Opinion Paragraph

In our opinion, the financial statements referred to above present fairly, in all material respects, the financial position of Westbrook Company, Inc. as of December 31, 2003 and 2002, and the results of its operations and its cash flows for each of the years in the three-year period ended December 31, 2003 in conformity with accounting principles generally accepted in the United States of America. Also, in our opinion, management's assertion on internal control over financial reporting referred to above is fairly stated, in all material respects, based on criteria established in *Internal Control-Integrated Framework* issued by the Committee of Sponsoring Organizations of the Treadway Commission (COSO).

Johnson and Wilson, LLP
March 6, 2004

multiple reporting periods on the financial statements. For management's assertion about the effectiveness of internal control, the report is as of the end of the most recent fiscal year.

If the auditor issues a separate report on internal control, the following paragraph should be added to the auditor's report on the financial statements:

> We have also audited in accordance with auditing standards generally accepted in the United States of America management's assertion that Westbrook Company, Inc. maintained effective internal control over financial reporting as of December 31, 2003, and our report dated March 6, 2004 expressed an unqualified opinion on that assertion.

The internal control report date should be the same as that of the financial statement opinion.

AUDITOR INDEPENDENCE

The SEC adopted rules strengthening auditor independence in January 2003 consistent with the requirements of Sarbanes-Oxley. The SEC rules focus on the following key aspects of independence:

- The prohibition of certain non-audit services
- The role of the audit committee in insulating the auditor from management pressure
- Potential conflicts of interest when auditors accept key management positions with the audit client
- The need for effective communications between the auditor and audit committee

Non-Audit Services

Consulting Services – The SEC's principles of independence for other services provided by auditors are based on three principles:

1. An auditor cannot function in the role of management
2. An auditor cannot audit his or her own work
3. An auditor cannot serve as an advocate for the client

Sarbanes-Oxley and the revised SEC rules restrict, but do not eliminate, the types of consulting services that can be provided to publicly held audit clients. Many of these services were prohibited under the existing SEC rules on independence adopted in November 2000. The new rules clarify many of the existing prohibitions, and expand the circumstances in which the services are prohibited.

Restricted Consulting Services Under
Sarbanes-Oxley and Revised SEC Rules

1. Bookkeeping and other accounting services
2. Financial information systems design and implementation
3. Appraisal or valuation services
4. Actuarial services
5. Internal audit outsourcing
6. Management or human resource functions
7. Broker or dealer or investment adviser, or investment banker services
8. Legal and expert services unrelated to the audit
9. Any other service that the PCAOB determines by regulation is impermissible.

Tax Services – Recent events involving IRS investigations of tax shelters recommended by accounting firms and the provision of tax services to key employees at Sprint and other companies illustrate that tax services can create a potential conflict of interest for the auditor in which the firm is in essence auditing its own work. Several major companies have placed restrictions on the use of their outside audit firm for certain types of tax services.

The SEC has reiterated its long-standing position that an accounting firm can provide tax services to audit clients without impairing independence. As a result, accountants can continue to provide tax services such as tax compliance, tax planning, and tax advice to clients. However, these services must receive audit committee pre-approval. In addition, companies must disclose the amount of fees paid for tax services. The SEC noted that certain tax services could in certain circumstances impair independence. In particular, the SEC recommends that audit committees carefully scrutinize use of their audit firm for a transaction recommended by the accountant that may have tax avoidance as its sole purpose and whose tax treatment may not be supported by the Internal Revenue Code.

Although the SEC has indicated that tax services are generally allowed, the PCAOB has authority to establish auditor independence rules. The PCAOB has indicated that it will revisit the issue of whether certain tax services affect independence, especially when auditors evaluate the consequences of tax shelters that the accounting firm recommended to the client.

Audit Committee Approval of Non-Audit Services – Non-audit services that are not prohibited by the Sarbanes-Oxley Act and the SEC rules must be pre-approved by the company's audit committee. In addition, an accountant is not independent of an audit client if an audit partner received compensation based on selling engagements to that client for services other than audit, review and attest services.

The employment of former audit team members with the audit client raises independence concerns. Consistent with the requirements of the Sarbanes-Oxley Act, the SEC has added a one-year "cooling off" period before a member of the audit engagement team can work for the client in certain key management positions. This has important implications for an auditor working for a CPA firm who receives an employment offer from the client, if it is publicly held, for a position as a chief executive officer, controller, chief financial officer, chief accounting officer or equivalent position. The CPA firm cannot continue to audit that client if the auditor accepts the position and has participated in any capacity in the audit for one year preceding the start of the audit. This does not affect the CPA firm's ability to continue the audit if the former auditor accepts a position such as assistant controller or accountant without primary accounting responsibilities.

Under SEC rules existing before Sarbanes-Oxley and continuing, an accounting firm is not independent with respect to an audit client if a former partner, principal, or shareholder, or professional employee of the firm accepts employment with a client if he or she has a continuing financial interest in the accounting firm, or is in a position to influence the accounting firm's operations or financial policies.

As required by Sarbanes-Oxley, the SEC independence rules require that the lead and concurring audit partner rotate off the audit engagement after a period of five years. Although not addressed in Sarbanes-Oxley, the SEC requires a five-year "time out" for the lead and concurring partners after rotation before they can return to that audit client. Additional audit partners with significant involvement on the audit must rotate after seven years and are subject to a two-year time out period.

Conflicts Arising from Employment Relationships

Partner Rotation

MANAGEMENT AND AUDITOR RESPONSIBILITIES

Management has always been responsible for the financial statements. Sarbanes-Oxley increases management's responsibility by requiring the chief executive officer (CEO) and chief financial officer (CFO) of public companies to certify the quarterly and annual financial statements submitted to the SEC. By signing those statements, management is certifying that the financial statements fully comply with the requirements of the Securities Exchange Act of 1934 and that the information contained in the report fairly presents, in all material respects, the financial condition and results of operations.

While financial statements filed with the SEC have previously included management's signatures, the responsibilities of the new CEO and CFO certifications are significantly increased. Sarbanes-Oxley contains criminal penalties for anyone who knowingly falsely certifies those statements. Criminal penalties include significant monetary fines or

Management's Responsibilities

imprisonment up to 20 years. To avoid these possibilities, most CEO's and CFO's of public companies are now devoting significant time to due diligence procedures conducted with other members of the management team before signing the certifications at each quarter and year end. The box below summarizes the six elements of management's certification.

Six Elements of Management's Certification of Financial Statements

1. Management has reviewed the financial statements.

2. Based on management's knowledge, the financial statements do not contain any untrue material fact or omit to state a material fact.

3. Based on management's knowledge, the financial statements and other financial information fairly present in all material respects the financial condition, results of operations, and cash flows of the company as of and for the period presented.

4. Management
    a. Is responsible for establishing and maintaining disclosure controls and procedures of the company.
    b. Has designed such disclosure programs and controls to ensure that material information is made known to them, particularly during the period in which the report is being prepared.
    c. Has evaluated the effectiveness of the company's disclosure controls and procedures as of a date within 90 days prior to the filing date of the report.
    d. Has presented in the report containing the financial statements their conclusions about the effectiveness of those disclosure controls and procedures based on the required evaluation as of that date.

5. Management has disclosed to its auditors and the audit committee
    a. All significant deficiencies in the design or operation of its internal control, which could adversely affect the company's ability to record, process, summarize and report financial data and have identified for the auditors any material weaknesses in internal controls.
    b. Any fraud, whether or not material, that involves management or other employees who have a significant role in the issuer's internal controls.

6. Management has indicated in the report containing the financial statements whether or not there were significant changes in internal controls or in other factors that could significantly affect internal controls subsequent to the date of management's evaluation, including any corrections to address significant deficiencies and material weaknesses.

Recall that, in addition to these certifications, Sarbanes-Oxley requires management to issue a report about its internal controls. As noted previously, the internal control report includes management's acknowledgement of its responsibility for establishing and maintaining adequate internal controls over financial reporting and its assessment of the effectiveness of those controls.

Auditors of public companies continue to be responsible for auditing the annual financial statements and for conducting timely reviews of quarterly financial statements. Sarbanes-Oxley adds to those responsibilities by requiring the auditor to attest to and report on management's assessment of the effectiveness of the company's internal controls over financial reporting.

In March 2003, the Auditing Standards Board issued an exposure draft of proposed standards to assist auditors in fulfilling this responsibility. The proposed standards direct the auditor to evaluate a company's entire system of internal control over financial reporting, including controls such as antifraud programs and controls. The proposals also allow auditors to either issue a separate attestation report on internal controls or combine that assessment about the effectiveness of internal controls with the auditor's report on the financial statements. There is uncertainty about whether this guidance will become final for public companies, given the PCAOB's decision to not delegate responsibility for auditing standards setting to the ASB. This is a top priority of the PCAOB.

The figure on the next page contains an example of the certification from Harley-Davidson, Inc.'s chief executive officer for the company's annual statements filed in the Form 10-K with the SEC. That example illustrates specific statements made by the chief executive officer for each of the six required elements of the certification noted previously. The CEO will make similar statements in the quarterly financial statements submitted in Form 10-Q's. In addition, the Forms 10-Q and 10-K filed with the SEC will contain similar certifications (not shown here) from Harley-Davidson's chief financial officer.

AUDIT EVIDENCE

According to auditing standards, audit documentation is the *records kept by the auditor of the procedures applied, the tests performed, the information obtained, and the pertinent conclusions reached in the engagement.* Chapter 7 of the text describes audit documentation as including all the information the auditor considers necessary to conduct the audit adequately and to provide support for the audit report.

The alleged document shredding by Andersen employees in the Enron investigation led to an intense focus on the importance of maintaining adequate documentation that provides the basis for the auditor's opinion on the financial statements. Sarbanes-Oxley requires the PCAOB to adopt an auditing standard requiring auditors to prepare and maintain for a period of not less than seven years, audit working papers and other information related to any audit report, in sufficient detail to support the auditor's conclusions. Sarbanes-Oxley makes the knowing and willful destruction of audit documentation within the seven year period a criminal offense subject to financial fines and imprisonment up to ten years.

Chief Executive Officer Certification

I, Jeffrey L. Bleustein, certify that:

1. I have reviewed this annual report on Form 10-K of Harley-Davidson, Inc.;

2. Based on my knowledge, this annual report does not contain any untrue statement of a material fact or omit to state a material fact necessary to make the statements made, in light of the circumstances under which such statements were made, not misleading with respect to the period covered by this annual report;

3. Based on my knowledge, the financial statements, and other financial information included in this annual report, fairly present in all material respects the financial condition, results of operations and cash flows of the registrant as of, and for, the periods presented in this annual report;

4. The registrant's other certifying officer and I are responsible for establishing and maintaining disclosure controls and procedures (as defined in Exchange Act Rules 13a-14 and 15d-14) for the registrant and have:

    (a) designed such disclosure controls and procedures to ensure that material information relating to the registrant, including its consolidated subsidiaries, is made known to us by others within those entities, particularly during the period in which this annual report is being prepared;

    (b) evaluated the effectiveness of the registrant's disclosure controls and procedures as of a date within 90 days prior to the filing date of this annual report (the "Evaluation Date"); and

    (c) presented in this annual report our conclusions about the effectiveness of the disclosure controls and procedures based on our evaluation as of the Evaluation Date;

5. The registrant's other certifying officer and I have disclosed, based on our most recent evaluation, to the registrant's auditors and the audit committee of registrant's board of directors (or persons performing the equivalent functions):

    (a) all significant deficiencies in the design or operation of internal controls which could adversely affect the registrant's ability to record, process, summarize and report financial data and have identified for the registrant's auditors any material weaknesses in internal controls; and

    (b) any fraud, whether or not material, that involves management or other employees who have a significant role in the registrant's internal controls; and

6. The registrant's other certifying officer and I have indicated in this annual report whether there were significant changes in internal controls or in other factors that could significantly affect internal controls subsequent to the date of our most recent evaluation, including any corrective actions with regard to significant deficiencies and material weaknesses.

Date: March 28, 2003
Jeffrey L. Bleustein
Chief Executive Officer

The Act delegated to the SEC responsibility for issuing further guidance about the nature and extent of documentation to be maintained. In February 2003, the SEC issued final rules on the retention of records for audits and reviews. The final rules require the auditor to maintain the following documentation:

- Working papers or other documents that form the basis for the audit of the company's annual financial statements or review of the company's quarterly financial statements.
- Memos, correspondence, communications, other documents, and records, including electronic records, that meet the following two criteria:
  (1) The materials are created, sent, or received in connection with the audit or review, and
  (2) The materials contain conclusions, opinions, analyses, or financial data related to the audit or review.

The SEC's rule significantly increases the audit documentation that must be retained. For example, auditors will now be required to retain email correspondence that contains information meeting the above criteria. These new requirements may affect the nature and extent of what auditors document during the audit.

The SEC's final rule acknowledges that administrative records and other documents not containing relevant financial data or the auditor's conclusions, opinions, or analyses do not meet the retention criteria. For example, superseded drafts of memos, duplicates, previous copies of working papers that have been corrected for typographical errors or errors due to training of new employees, or voice-mail messages do not need to be retained.

CLIENT ACCEPTANCE AND CONTINUANCE

Auditors have historically viewed management as "the client," despite the fact that most public companies require shareholder approval of the auditor's selection. Management works directly with the auditor in coordinating the audit, including audit fee negotiation. Auditor objectivity may be threatened when they perceive management as the client with primary authority to hire and fire the auditor.

To address this concern, Sarbanes-Oxley explicitly shifts responsibility for hiring and firing of the auditor from management to the audit committee for public companies. Now, the audit committee is responsible for pre-approving all audit and non-audit services. Specifically, the audit committee is responsible for the appointment, compensation, and oversight of the work of the auditor, including

Defining "The Client"

resolution of disagreements between management and the auditor for financial reporting. And, as noted previously, auditors are responsible for communicating certain matters identified during the audit to the audit committee. The intent of these new provisions is to redefine "the client" as being the audit committee, not management.

This shift has implications for audit planning. As noted in Chapter 8, auditors are already responsible for establishing an understanding with the client regarding services to be performed in the audit engagement. Often that understanding is established through an engagement letter signed by management. Auditors should now establish this understanding with the audit committee and document that understanding in the audit files. In some cases, auditors may obtain signed engagement letters directly from the audit committee.

In March 2003, the ASB issued an exposure draft of a proposed SAS titled, *Sarbanes-Oxley Omnibus Statement on Auditing Standards,* that revises existing guidance for establishing an understanding with the client. Part of that proposed standard redefines many of the specific matters to be addressed when obtaining the understanding with the client that will now be established with the audit committee. The ASB is in the process of incorporating comments received during the exposure period and will forward the revised draft guidance to the PCAOB for final consideration and issuance.

Evaluation of Related Party Transactions

Chapter 8 defines a related party transaction as any transaction between the client and a related party. Related parties include an affiliated company, a principal owner of the client company, or any other party with which the client deals where one or more of the parties can influence the management or operating policies of the other. Related party transactions have always been viewed as inherently risky because they are not at arms length and may not be valued at the same amount as they would have been if the transactions had been with an independent third party. Most auditors assess inherent risk as high for related parties and related party transactions.

Because of the lack of independence between the parties involved, Sarbanes-Oxley prohibits related party transactions that involve personal loans to executives. It is now unlawful for any public company to extend or maintain credit, to arrange for the extension of credit, or to renew the extension of credit in the form of a personal loan to any director or executive officer of the company. These restrictions do not apply to any loan, such as a home loan or credit card agreement, made by a bank or other insured financial institution under normal banking operations using market terms offered to the general public. In light of these prohibitions, auditors should be alert for any such loans to executives or other employees to ensure those transactions do not exist and if they do, to deal with them as illegal acts.

As part of the auditor's planning procedures to obtain an understanding of the client's business and industry, auditors evaluate the strategies and business processes used by management and the board of directors to oversee and govern the client's business. Matters related to management's philosophy and operating style are particularly relevant to the auditor's evaluation.

Companies frequently communicate the entity's values and ethical standards through policy statements and codes of conduct. In response to requirements in the Sarbanes-Oxley Act, the SEC now requires each public company to disclose whether it has adopted a code of ethics that applies to senior management, including the CEO, CFO, and principal accounting officer or controller. A company that has not adopted such a code must disclose this fact and explain why it has not done so. The SEC also requires companies to promptly disclose amendments and waivers to the code of ethics for any of those officers. The boxed items below summarize the elements that should be included in a public company's code of ethics.

Required Elements of the Code of Ethics

A Code of Ethics must include written standards that are reasonably designed to deter wrongdoing and to promote:

- Honest and ethical conduct, including the ethical handling of actual or apparent conflicts of interest between personal and professional relationships;

- Full, fair, accurate, timely, and understandable disclosure in reports and documents that a public company files with the SEC or includes in other public communications;

- Compliance with applicable governmental laws, rules, and regulations;

- Prompt internal reporting to an appropriate person identified in the code of violations of the code; and

- Accountability for adherence to the code.

As a part of the understanding of the client's governance system, auditors should gain knowledge of the company's code of ethics. In particular, auditors should examine any changes and waivers of the code of conduct made for employees for implications about the governance system and related integrity and ethical values of senior management.

Assess Client Business Risk   Chapter 8 highlights procedures auditors perform to obtain an understanding of the client's business and industry, which the auditor uses to assess client business risk. The auditor's primary concern is to identify risks that may increase the likelihood of material misstatements in the financial statements.

Management is a primary source for identifying client business risks. To be in position to certify quarterly and annual financial statements and to evaluate the effectiveness of disclosure controls and procedures now required by Sarbanes-Oxley, management should conduct thorough evaluations of relevant client business risks affecting financial reporting.

One certification is that management has designed disclosure controls and procedures to ensure that material information is made known to them. The SEC believes these procedures are intended to cover a broader range of information than is covered by an issuer's internal controls for financial reporting. In the SEC's view, the procedures should capture information that is relevant to assess the need to disclose developments and *risks* that pertain to the company's business. Inquiries of management about client business risks identified by them in advance of certifying quarterly and annual financial statements may provide a significant source of information for auditors about client business risks affecting financial reporting.

Another element of the certifications is that management has notified the auditors and the audit committee of any significant deficiencies in internal control, including material weaknesses. Such information is useful to auditors as they evaluate the impact of internal control on the likelihood of material misstatements in financial statements.

INTERNAL CONTROL AND CONTROL RISK

Chapter 10 outlines the auditor's responsibility for internal controls in a financial statement audit. Under Sarbanes-Oxley, auditors will continue to obtain an understanding of internal controls in every audit to assess control risk. However, they will also perform other procedures to report on management's assertion about internal controls.

Understanding internal controls and tests of controls performed solely for the purpose of expressing an opinion on the financial statements are normally not sufficient for expressing an opinion on internal controls. In an audit of the financial statements, auditors obtain an understanding of internal control to assess control risk. The extent of testing the controls varies depending on assessed control risk. For example, when control risk is assessed below the maximum, the auditor designs and performs a combination of tests of controls and substantive procedures. On the other hand, when control risk is assessed at maximum, the auditor performs only substantive procedures.

In contrast, the range of controls to be tested by auditors to express an opinion on internal controls is often significantly broader than that tested solely to express an opinion on the financial statements. To express an opinion on internal controls, the auditor obtains an understanding of and performs tests of controls for *all* significant account balances, classes of transactions, and disclosures and related assertions in the financial statements. Those controls may not have been tested in a financial statement audit. The following figure illustrates the differences in controls tested in an audit of internal controls from controls tested in an audit of the financial statements.

**Differences in Scope of Controls Tested in an Audit
of Internal Control and an Audit of Financial Statements**

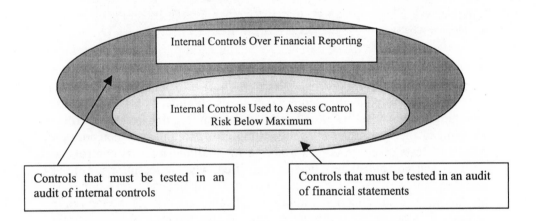

The level of assurance obtained from tests of controls in an audit of internal controls also typically differs from the level of assurance obtained from tests of controls in an audit of financial statements. Tests of controls performed in an audit of internal control must be sufficient to obtain a high level of assurance about their operating effectiveness. Tests of controls performed in a financial statement audit may provide only moderate or low assurance about their operating effectiveness, given that other assurance is obtained from substantive procedures. Thus, the nature, timing, and extent of tests of controls in an audit of internal control are likely to be greater than tests of controls performed in a financial statement audit. The figure on the following page illustrates the differences in the types of procedures performed to serve as the basis for the opinion on internal controls and the opinion on the financial statements.

Comparison of Audit of Internal Control and Audit of Financial Statements

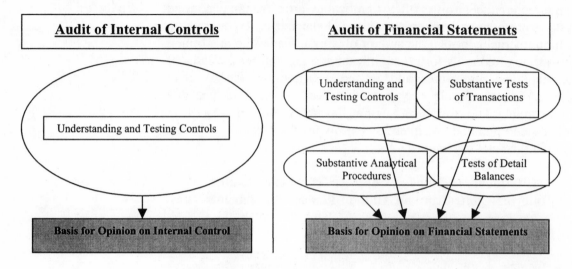

While the nature, timing and extent of testing controls differ between an audit of financial statements and the audit of internal controls, auditors can use the knowledge about internal controls obtained as part of the audit of internal controls as the basis for the understanding of internal control in an audit of the financial statements. Similarly, auditors may consider the results of tests of controls performed in the audit of internal controls, as well as internal control deficiencies identified, when assessing control risk and designing substantive procedures for the financial statement audit.

Because of the inherent limitations of internal control, the degree of reliance that can be placed by the auditor on internal control to reduce the likelihood of material misstatements in the financial statements is limited, regardless of the effectiveness of internal control. Auditors of the financial statements must continue to perform substantive procedures for each material account and class of transactions. The extent of evidence obtained about the operating effectiveness of internal controls in an audit of internal controls does not eliminate the requirement for the auditor to perform substantive procedures in the financial statement audit.

Evidence the auditor obtains from performing substantive procedures in an audit of the financial statements should be considered by the auditor when auditing internal controls. When substantive procedures detect material misstatements, the auditor should consider whether that evidence affects judgments about the effectiveness of internal controls. Material misstatements detected by the auditor that were not identified by the client ordinarily indicate the existence of a material weakness in internal control.

One likely change in the audit of public companies as a result of the requirement for the audit of internal controls is an increased reliance on internal control in financial statement audits. Previously, it was often cost effective to perform increased substantive tests instead of tests of controls in some or all cycles even if controls were effective. Now, the auditor is likely to rely on these controls because they must be tested in the audit of internal controls anyway.

22

One of the five components of internal control is the control environment. Chapter 10 in the text notes that the control environment consists of the actions, policies, and procedures that reflect the overall attitudes of top management, directors, and the owners of the entity about internal control and its importance to the entity.

An important subcomponent of the control environment is board of director and audit committee participation. The board is charged with providing regular assessments of management-established internal control. And, it provides active and objective oversight to reduce the risk of likelihood of management override of internal controls. An effective board of directors is independent of management.

To assist the board in its oversight, the board creates an audit committee that is charged with oversight responsibility for the financial reporting process. Sarbanes-Oxley requires that each member of the audit committee be a member of the board of directors and be independent of management. To be considered independent, the audit committee member cannot accept any consulting, advisory, or other compensation from the company except for the compensation as a board and audit committee member.

Sarbanes-Oxley also directed the SEC to issue final rules requiring public companies to disclose whether or not the audit committee includes at least one member who is a financial expert. In January 2003, the SEC issued its final rule that defines an audit committee financial expert as a person who has the following attributes:

- An understanding of generally accepted accounting principles and financial statements;
- The ability to assess the general application of such principles in connection with the accounting for estimates, accruals, and reserves;
- Experience preparing, auditing, analyzing, or evaluating financial statements that present a breadth and level of complexity of accounting issues that are generally comparable to the breadth and complexity of issues that can reasonably be expected to be raised by the company's financial statements, or experience supervising one or more persons engaged in such activities;
- An understanding of internal controls and procedures for financial reporting; and
- An understanding of audit committee functions.

The boxed information on the following page summarizes one or more ways a potential audit committee member can acquire the above attributes.

- Education and experience as a principal financial officer, principal accounting officer, controller, public accountant or auditor, or experiences in one or more positions that involve the performance of similar functions;

- Experience actively supervising the principal financial officer, principal accounting officer, controller, public accountant, auditor or person performing similar functions;

- Experience overseeing or assessing the performance of companies or public accountants in the preparation, auditing, or evaluation of financial statements; or

- Other relevant experience.

In addition to requiring public companies to disclose whether they have at least one audit committee financial expert, the SEC final rules also require disclosure of the name of the expert, if one exists, and whether the expert is independent of management. A company that does not have an audit committee financial expert must disclose this fact and explain why it has no such expert.

The national stock exchanges have also made recent changes to the listing requirements for companies whose securities trade on those exchanges. For example, the New York Stock Exchange changed listing requirements designed to strengthen corporate governance and disclosure. Among the many changes, the NYSE now requires the chair of the audit committee of NYSE registrants to have accounting or financial management experience, and listed companies must have an audit committee, nominating committee, and compensation committee each comprised solely of independent directors.

Auditors should use this enhanced disclosure about characteristics of client boards of directors and related committees, such as the audit committee, to assess the strength of the client's control environment. To the extent that the characteristics exceed minimum requirements of the SEC and national stock exchanges, auditors may conclude that the company's control environment has improved.

COMPLETING THE AUDIT

Obtain Management Representation Letter

Professional auditing standards require the auditor to obtain a letter of representation documenting management's most important oral representations during the audit. Chapter 23 in the text notes that there are two primary purposes for obtaining the letter of representation (see top of next page):

1. To impress upon management its responsibility for the assertions in the financial statements.
2. To document the responses from management to inquiries about various aspects of the audit.

Existing professional standards suggests four categories of specific matters to be included in the letter of representation:

1. Financial statements
2. Completeness of information
3. Recognition, measurement, and disclosure
4. Subsequent events

The proposed *Sarbanes-Oxley Omnibus Statement on Auditing Standards* issued by the ASB in March 2003 includes a proposed fifth category that deals with internal control. The specific representations in that category are summarized in the box below. Auditors of public companies may wish to obtain a combined representation letter for both the audit of the financial statements and the audit of internal control.

Representations About Internal Controls

- Disclosure of all significant deficiencies, including material weaknesses, in the design or operation of internal controls that could adversely affect the entity's ability to record, process, summarize, and report financial data.

- Management's acknowledgement of its responsibility for the design and implementation of programs and controls to prevent and detect fraud.

- Knowledge of fraud or suspected fraud affecting the entity involving (1) management, (2) employees who have significant roles in internal control, or (3) others where the fraud could have a material effect on the financial statements.

- Knowledge of any allegations of fraud or suspected fraud affecting the entity obtained through communications from employees, former employees, analysts, regulators, short sellers, or others.

Communicate with the Audit Committee and Management

Auditing professional standards already include responsibilities to communicate certain matters to the audit committee. Sarbanes-Oxley expands those requirements by also requiring the auditor to timely report the following items to the audit committee (see top of next page):

- All critical accounting policies and practices to be used.
- All alternative treatments of financial information within generally accepted accounting principles that have been discussed with management, ramifications of the use of such alternative disclosures and treatments, and the treatment preferred by the auditor; and
- Other material written communications between the auditor and management, such as any management letter or schedule of unadjusted differences.

As the audit is completed, the auditor should determine that the audit committee is informed about the initial selection of and changes in significant accounting policies or their application during the current audit period. When changes have occurred, the auditor should inform the committee of the reasons for the change. The auditor should also communicate information about methods used to account for significant unusual transactions and the effect of significant accounting policies in controversial or emerging areas.

SAS NO. 99, *CONSIDERATION OF FRAUD IN A FINANCIAL STATEMENT AUDIT*

The ASB issued SAS No. 99, *Consideration of Fraud in a Financial Statement Audit*, in December 2002. The standard supersedes SAS No. 82 in providing guidance to auditors in fulfilling their responsibility for detecting fraud in an audit of financial statements. Although the occurrence of several high-profile alleged cases of fraudulent financial reporting provided primary motivation for the issuance of Sarbanes-Oxley, the ASB's efforts to issue SAS No. 99 were well underway before the issuance of the Act.

Chapters 6 and 9 of the text are based on SAS No. 99. The following sections include some of the material on fraud from the text plus additional detail on the guidance in SAS No. 99.

Errors Versus Fraud

SAS 99 distinguishes between two types of misstatements: errors and fraud. Either type of misstatement can be material or immaterial. An *error* is an *unintentional* misstatement of the financial statements, whereas *fraud* is *intentional*. Two examples of errors are a mistake in extending prices times quantity on a sales invoice and overlooking older raw materials in determining the lower or cost of market for inventory.

For fraud, there is a distinction between *misappropriation of assets*, often called defalcation or employee fraud, and *fraudulent financial reporting*, often called management fraud. An example of misappropriation of assets is a clerk taking cash at the time a sale is made and not entering the sale in the cash register. An example of fraudulent financial reporting is the intentional overstatement of sales near the balance sheet date to increase reported earnings.

Auditing standards make no distinction between the auditor's responsibility for searching for errors and fraud, whether from fraudulent financial reporting or misappropriation of assets. For both errors and fraud, the auditor must obtain reasonable assurance about whether the statements are free of material misstatements.

The standards also recognize that it is often more difficult to detect fraud than errors because management or the employees perpetrating the fraud *attempt to conceal the fraud*. The difficulty of detection does not change the auditor's responsibility to properly plan and perform the audit.

Assessing Fraud Risks

To meet their fraud detection responsibilities, auditors obtain information to assess the risk of fraud arising from fraudulent financial reporting and misappropriations of assets. Auditors gather information to determine the extent that fraud conditions exist. As discussed in Chapter 9 of the text, the three conditions of fraud described in SAS No. 99 are:

1. *Incentives/Pressures*. Management or other employees have incentives or pressures to commit fraud.
2. *Opportunities*. Circumstances provide opportunities for management or employees to commit fraud.
3. *Attitudes/Rationalization*. An attitude, character, or set of ethical values exist that allow management or employees to commit a dishonest act or they are in an environment that imposes sufficient pressure that causes them to rationalize committing a dishonest act.

These three conditions are often referred to as the "fraud triangle."

The Fraud Triangle

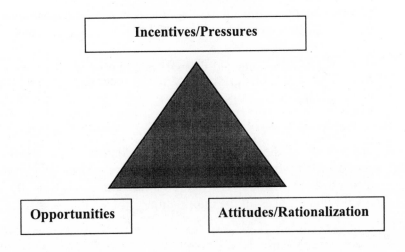

Forensic experts believe the evaluation of information about fraud is enhanced when it is considered in the context of these three conditions. Considering the possibility of fraud along these dimensions provides auditors with a helpful framework for obtaining and evaluating information about the risks of material misstatements due to fraud.

The table on the following page (Table 9-4 from the text) provides examples of fraud risk factors for each of the three conditions of fraud for fraudulent financial reporting.

Information Affecting Risk of Fraud

Auditors have historically used fraud risk factor checklists as their primary source of information about fraud risks. Based on the belief that auditor processes for identifying and assessing fraud risks needed to be improved, SAS No. 99 significantly expands the requirements and guidance for gathering information about the risks of fraud. The emphasis is on obtaining a broader set of information as the source of input about fraud risks that is beyond simply considering fraud risk factors. Considering all information about risks, not just the risk factors, should improve the auditor's ability to identify and assess those risks, and aid in designing appropriate audit procedures.

Chapter 9 summarizes this expanded set of information gathered to assess fraud risk. Auditors now consider the following:

- Information obtained from experienced audit team members about their knowledge of the company and its industry, including how and where the company might be susceptible to material misstatements due to fraud.
- Responses to auditor inquiries of management about their views about the risks of fraud and about existing programs and controls to address specific identified fraud risks.
- Specific risk factors related to fraudulent financial reporting and misappropriations of assets.
- Analytical procedures results obtained during planning that indicate possible implausible or unexpected analytical relationships.
- Knowledge obtained through such things as client acceptance and retention decisions, interim review of financial statements, and the consideration of fraud risks.

The auditor considers all the information gathered through the performance of these procedures in the context of the three conditions present when fraud exists: incentives/pressures, opportunities, and attitudes/rationalization. The figure on the bottom of page 30 summarizes how the auditor uses all the information gathered to assess fraud risks.

Examples of Risk Factors for Fraudulent Financial Reporting

THREE CONDITIONS OF FRAUD

Incentives/Pressures

Management or other employees have incentives or pressures to materially misstate financial statements.

Examples of Risk Factors

- Financial stability or profitability is threatened by economic, industry, or entity operating conditions. Examples include significant declines in customer demand and increasing business failures in either the industry or overall economy.

- Excessive pressure for management to meet debt repayment or other debt covenant requirements.

- Management or the board of directors' personal net worth is materially threatened by the entity's financial performance.

Opportunities

Circumstances provide an opportunity for management or employees to misstate financial statements.

Examples of Risk Factors

- Significant accounting estimates involve subjective judgments or uncertainties that are difficult to verify.

- Ineffective board of director or audit committee oversight over financial reporting.

- High turnover or ineffective accounting, internal audit, or information technology staff.

Attitudes/Rationalization

An attitude, character, or set of ethical values exists that allows management or employees to intentionally commit a dishonest act, or they are in an environment that imposes sufficient pressure that causes them to rationalize committing a dishonest act.

Examples of Risk Factors

- Inappropriate or ineffective communication and support of the entity's values.

- Known history of violations of securities laws or other laws and regulations.

- Management's practice of making overly aggressive or unrealistic forecasts to analysts, creditors, and other third parties.

Communications Among Engagement Personnel – As depicted in the diagram on the bottom of this page, a dialogue held among the audit team about fraud risks serves as one of the sources of information auditors use to assess fraud risks. SAS No. 99 requires the audit team to conduct these discussions to share insights from more experienced audit team members and to "brainstorm" ideas that address the following:

- How and where they believe the entity's financial statements might be susceptible to material misstatement due to fraud. This should include consideration of known external and internal factors affecting the entity that might
  - Create an incentive or pressure for management to commit fraud.
  - Provide the opportunity for fraud to be perpetrated.
  - Indicate a culture or environment that enables management to rationalize fraudulent acts.
- How management could perpetrate and conceal fraudulent financial reporting.
- How assets of the entity could be misappropriated.
- How the auditor might respond to the susceptibility of material misstatements due to fraud.

Sources of Information Gathered to Assess Fraud Risks

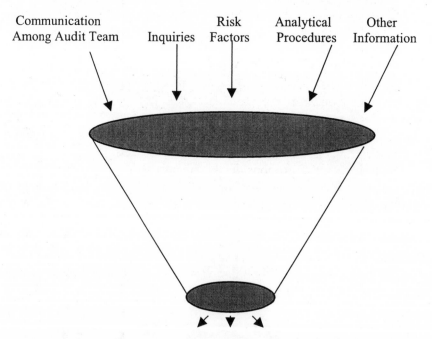

Identified Risks of Material Misstatements Due to Fraud

Focus on Professional Skepticism – SAS No. 1 states that, in exercising professional skepticism, an auditor *"neither assumes that management is dishonest nor assumes unquestioned honesty."* In practice, maintaining this attitude of "neutrality" can be difficult because, despite allegations in some recent high profile cases, material frauds are still relatively rare compared to the number of audits of financial statements conducted annually. In fact, most auditors will never encounter a material fraud during their careers. Also, through rigorous client acceptance and continuance evaluation procedures, auditors reject most potential clients perceived as lacking appropriate levels of honesty and integrity.

SAS No. 99 places stronger emphasis on the auditor's consideration of a client's susceptibility to fraud, regardless of the auditor's beliefs about the likelihood of fraud and management's honesty and integrity. Specifically, the standard requires that during audit planning in every audit, the engagement team must discuss the need to maintain a questioning mind throughout the audit in identifying fraud risks and to critically evaluate audit evidence.

- **Questioning Mind:** In maintaining a "questioning mind" auditors should set aside any prior beliefs about management's integrity and honesty. In this regard, the discussion should include consideration of the potential for management override of controls.
- **Critical Evaluation of Audit Evidence:** Auditors should thoroughly probe the issues, acquire additional evidence as necessary, and consult with other team members rather than rationalize or dismiss information or other conditions that indicate a material misstatement due to fraud may have occurred.

Responding to the Risks of Fraud

When risks of material misstatements due to fraud are identified, the auditor should first discuss these findings with management and obtain management's views of the potential fraud and existing programs and controls designed to prevent or detect misstatements. Management may have programs and controls designed to mitigate specific risks of fraud or broader programs designed to prevent, deter, and detect fraud.

Auditors should then consider whether such programs and controls mitigate the identified risks of material misstatements due to fraud or whether specific control deficiencies exacerbate the risks. When assessing the risks of material misstatement due to fraud, the auditor considers whether programs and controls are suitably designed and placed in operation.

Chapter 9 summarizes the three ways auditors respond to fraud risks as including the following (see top of next page):

1. Design and perform audit procedures to address identified risks.
2. Change the overall conduct of the audit to respond to identified fraud risks.
3. Perform procedures to address the risk of management override of controls.

The last of these three responses recognizes that the risk of management override of controls exists in virtually all audits and can manifest itself in a number of unpredictable ways. Because management is in a unique position to perpetrate fraud by overriding established controls that would otherwise appear to be operating effectively, auditors must now perform procedures in every audit to further address the risk of management override of controls. Three procedures must be performed in every audit:

1. **Examine journal entries and other adjustments for evidence of possible misstatements due to fraud.** SAS No. 99 requires testing journal entries and other financial statement adjustments because fraud often involves the recording of inappropriate or unauthorized journal entries throughout the year or at period end. Fraud often results from adjustments to amounts reported in the financial statements even when there are effective internal controls in the rest of the recording processes. The auditor is required to:

   - Obtain an understanding of the entity's financial reporting process and the controls over journal entries and other adjustments.
   - Identify and select journal entries and other adjustments for testing.
   - Determine the timing of the testing.
   - Inquire of individuals involved in the financial reporting process about inappropriate or unusual activity in processing journal entries and other adjustments.

2. **Review accounting estimates for biases.** Fraudulent financial reporting is often accomplished through intentional misstatement of accounting estimates. SAS No. 99 requires the auditor to consider the potential for management bias when reviewing current year estimates. It requires a "look back" at significant prior year estimates to identify any changes in the company's process or management's judgments and assumptions that might indicate a potential bias. For example, management's estimates may have been clustered at the high end of the range of acceptable amounts in the prior year and clustered at the low end of the range in the current year.

3. **Evaluate the business rationale for significant unusual transactions.** SAS No. 99 places greater focus on understanding the underlying business rationale for significant unusual transactions that might be outside the normal course of business for the company, given the auditor's understanding of the entity and its environment. The auditor should gain an understanding of the business rationale and whether that rationale suggests that the transactions have been entered into to engage in fraudulent financial reporting. For example, the auditor should determine whether accounting treatment benefits are management's sole reason for engaging in the transactions.

Evaluating Audit Evidence

The auditor's assessment of the risks of material misstatement due to fraud should be ongoing throughout the audit. Conditions may be identified during fieldwork that change or support a judgment about the assessment of fraud risks. For example, the auditor should be alert for the following conditions:

- Discrepancies in the accounting records.
- Conflicting or missing evidential matter.
- Problematic or unusual relationships between the auditor and management.
- Results from substantive or final review stage analytical procedures that indicate a previously unrecognized fraud risk.
- Responses to inquiries made throughout the audit that have been vague or implausible, or that have produced evidence that is inconsistent with other evidence.

Documentation

SAS No. 99 expands the documentation requirements beyond that previously required. Auditors must document the following related to the auditor's consideration of material misstatements due to fraud:

- The discussion among engagement team personnel in planning the audit regarding the susceptibility of the entity's financial statements to material misstatements due to fraud. Documentation should include
    - How and when the discussion occurred;
    - Description of audit team members who participated; and
    - Subject matter discussed.
- Procedures performed to obtain information necessary to identify and assess the risks of material misstatements due to fraud.
- Specific risks of material misstatements due to fraud that were identified, and a description of the auditor's response to those risks.
- Reasons supporting the auditor's conclusion, if the auditor has not identified in a particular circumstance improper revenue recognition as a risk of material misstatement due to fraud.

- Results of the procedures performed to further address the risk of management override of controls.
- Other conditions and analytical relationships that caused the auditor to believe that additional auditing procedures or other responses were required and any further responses the auditor concluded were appropriate to address such risks or other conditions.
- The nature of communications about fraud made to management, the audit committee, or others.

AUDITOR'S RISK ASSESSMENT AND RISK RESPONSE PROCESSES

In December 2002, the ASB issued an exposure draft of seven proposed SASs relating to the auditor's risk assessment process. The ASB's primary objective is to enhance auditors' application of the audit risk model in practice by requiring:

- More in-depth understanding of the entity and its environment, including its internal control, to identify the risks of material misstatement in the financial statements and what the entity is doing to mitigate them.
- More rigorous assessment of the risks of material misstatement of the financial statements based on that understanding.
- Improved linkage between the assessed risks and the nature, timing, and extent of audit procedures performed in response to those risks.

Many of the concepts related to obtaining an in-depth understanding of the client's business and environment are integrated throughout the text. Chapter 8 on audit planning highlights the importance of understanding the client's business and industry to identify client business risks that may ultimately lead to increased likelihood of material misstatements in financial statements. The process of obtaining an understanding of key client business objectives and strategies to identify related client business risks is integrated throughout the remaining chapters that address specific transaction cycle issues. As a result, the spirit of these seven proposed SASs is currently integrated throughout the text.

There are more specific aspects of the proposed SASs that, if approved, will impact various requirements in current professional standards. Next is a highlight of how the specific proposals will change the audit process, if approved (see top of next page):

- **Expands the quality and depth of the auditor's required understanding of the entity and its environment, including its internal control.** The proposed standards require the auditor to obtain an understanding of a significantly expanded set of information about specific elements of the entity and its environment. The purpose is to enhance the auditor's ability to identify and assess risks that may lead to material misstatements in the financial statements. For example, the auditor will obtain information from management about the nature of its operations, ownership structure, current objectives and strategies, and related business risks in an effort to identify potential risks of material financial statement misstatements. The auditor is required to perform risk assessment procedures in all audits to obtain an understanding, including updated information obtained in prior audits that the auditor intends to use in the current audit. The expanded understanding about the client and its environment should also be helpful to the auditor throughout the audit when making judgments about materiality and when critically evaluating audit evidence.

- **Requires the auditor to assess the risks of material misstatements at the financial statement level and at the assertion level on all audits based on the understanding obtained.** The proposed changes note that assessing risks of material misstatements encompasses a combined assessment of inherent risk and control risk. The proposed changes eliminate the auditor's ability to assess "risk at the maximum" without support for that assessment. Thus, auditors will be required to support all risk assessments at whatever level, including risks at the maximum. In addition, the proposed SASs require the auditor to identify "significant risks" that require special audit consideration, and risks for which substantive procedures alone will not reduce audit risk to an appropriate level.

- **Eliminates the "default to maximum" for control risk, which should encourage testing of controls.** Auditors will no longer be able to assess control risk "at the maximum" without support for that assessment. Thus, that kind of audit approach can no longer be used as a default audit strategy. Instead, auditors must document the basis for a control risk at maximum assessment. The ASB believes this will encourage the testing of controls in all audits. In addition, the proposed changes expand the auditor's requirement to understand internal controls in every audit by also requiring the auditor to evaluate the design of controls, including relevant control procedures, over "significant risks," and to determine whether those control procedures have been implemented.

- **Emphasizes importance of the entity's risk assessment process.** The proposed SASs emphasize that when the auditor identifies potential risks of material misstatements in the financial statements, it is important for the auditor to consider the entity's risk assessment process. To assist the auditor with this consideration, the proposed SASs discuss how the entity's risk assessment process fits in with the entity's process of setting objectives and strategies and assessing related business risks. When the auditor identifies risks of material misstatements that the entity's risk assessment processes failed to detect, the proposed SASs require the auditor to consider why the process failed and whether the process is appropriate in the circumstance.

- **Strengthens the linkage between assessed risks and the auditor's responses to those risks.** Because auditors frequently struggle with designing an appropriate audit response to identified risks, the proposed SASs contain expanded guidance designed to significantly improve the auditor's ability to effectively address identified risks. Auditors are required to determine both an overall response to address the risks of material misstatements at the financial statement level and a response to assess risks of material misstatements at the assertion level. The proposed guidance emphasizes the importance of the nature of the audit procedures in responding to assessed risks. The proposed SASs also require the auditor to perform substantive procedures for "significant risks." These substantive procedures consist of tests of details alone or tests of details combined with substantive analytical procedures that are specifically responsive to the identified risks. If the auditor plans to rely on the operating effectiveness of controls to mitigate a significant risk, the auditor is required to obtain all evidence about the operating effectiveness of those controls from tests of controls performed in the current period. This means that the auditor cannot conclude that they are operating effectively based on tests of controls performed in prior audits even if the auditor determined the controls did not change since that testing.

- **Clarifies the auditor's ability to rely on audit evidence gathered in prior audits.** Except for controls related to significant risks, the auditor may rely on controls that have not changed since they were last tested. But, the auditor must perform tests of the operating effectiveness of those controls at least every third audit.

- **Strengthens guidance for testing disclosures.** The proposed SASs include expanded guidance to specifically address the importance of considering the completeness of disclosures and their understandability. The assertions related to presentation and disclosure have been significantly revised to provide this emphasis.

- **Expands documentation requirements.** Because the ASB believes that documentation requirements can drive behavior, the proposed SASs require the auditor to document, among other things, the following items:
    - Results of the risk assessments both at the financial statement level and the assertion levels;
    - The nature, timing, and extent of audit procedures performed;
    - The linkage of auditor responses with the assessed risks at the assertion level; and
    - Results of the audit procedures.

Now that the PCAOB has assumed responsibility for setting auditing standards applicable to audits of public company financial statements, there is uncertainty as to whether these provisions will ultimately be adopted. The ASB plans to forward the exposure drafts and related comment letters to the PCAOB for further evaluation. There is also consideration of the AICPA continuing to issue auditing standards for private companies.

CHANGES IN THE CPA EXAM

The final paper-and-pencil Uniform CPA examination will be given on November 5 and 6, 2003. The computer-based exam format will be delivered beginning April 5, 2004. The change to a computer-based examination will be accompanied by significant changes in exam delivery, content, and format. The exam will be delivered by Prometric at more than 300 testing centers. Instead of a single exam, candidates will take different, but equivalent exams drawn from a pool of test questions.

Exam length – The revised exam will consist of four sections, with a total examination length of 14 hours.

Exam Length and Scheduling

Time Breakdowns by Section for Revised Uniform CPA Examination				
Examination Length (hours)	Auditing & Attestation	Financial Accounting & Reporting	Regulation	Business Environment & Concepts
14	4.5	4	3	2.5

Source: The *CPA Exam Alert*, May/June 2002

Exam scheduling – The computer-based exam format will be much more flexible for candidates. The computer exam will be offered up to six days per week, and will be offered two out of every three months throughout the year. In addition, the AICPA Board of Examiners has recommended that candidates be allowed to take the sections individually, in any order, or all at one time. Currently, most states require first time candidates to sit for the entire exam.

Candidates must pass all four sections of the exam in a rolling 18-month period that begins on the date the first section passed is taken. If all four sections are not passed within the 18-month period, credits for any section passed outside the 18-month window expire and that section must be retaken.

Exam Format and Content

Exam format – The exam will consist of 80% multiple-choice questions. The remaining 20% will consist of one or two simulations in each section. Simulations are case studies that will test candidates accounting and auditing skills using real life work-related situations. The changes in exam format are designed to reflect changes in the work performed by entry-level CPAs. The revised exam recognizes the integral role of technology and the need for higher-order skills.

Simulations will be approximately 20-40 minutes in length. Most simulations will contain research activities, such as an electronic search of authoritative literature. In the auditing & attestation section, the research may also include accessing audit documentation or annual reports. Examination candidates are also expected to know how to use common spreadsheet and word processing functions. They must also be able to use a financial calculator or spreadsheet to perform financial calculations. A tutorial is available on the CPA exam Web site that covers the revised examination's format and navigation functions to familiarize candidates with the types of questions used in the computer-based test. The CPA exam Web site is *www.cpa-exam.org*.

Exam Content – The following describes the four sections of the computer-based examination:

- *Auditing & Attestation* – This section covers knowledge of auditing procedures, generally accepted auditing standards and other standards related to attest engagements, and the skills needed to apply that knowledge in those engagements.
- *Financial Accounting & Reporting* – This section covers knowledge of generally accepted accounting principles for businesses, not-for-profit organizations, and governmental entities, and the skills needed to apply that knowledge.
- *Regulation* – This section covers knowledge of federal taxation, ethics, professional and legal responsibilities, and business law, and the skills needed to apply that knowledge.

- *Business Environment & Concepts* – This section covers knowledge of the general business environment and business concepts that candidates need to know in order to understand the underlying business reasons for and accounting implications of business transactions, and the skills needed to apply that knowledge.

Transition rules – Candidates who have earned credits on the pencil-and-paper exam will be given credits for corresponding sections on the computer-based exam as indicated in the following table.

Paper-and-Pencil Examination Section	Computer-Based Examination Section
Auditing	Auditing & Attestation
Financial Accounting & Reporting (FARE)	Financial Accounting & Reporting
Accounting & Reporting (ARE)	Regulation
Business Law & Professional Responsibilities (LPR)	Business Environment & Concepts

Source: The *CPA Exam Alert*, May/June 2002

REVIEW QUESTIONS

1. Explain why several large accounting firms disposed of their consulting practices. Did the Sarbanes-Oxley Act play a role in these decisions?

2. What is the largest source of revenue for the Big 4 accounting firms? What was the likely largest source of revenue for these firms three years ago?

3. Who is responsible for establishing auditing standards for audits of public companies? Who is responsible for establishing accounting standards for public companies? Explain.

4. How many paragraphs are in a combined auditor's report on financial statements and internal control? What is the nature of the additional paragraph?

5. In a report on internal control, does the auditor's report cover internal control for a period or at a point of time? What date should be used for the auditor's report on internal control?

6. To what extent do the Sarbanes-Oxley Act and revised SEC independence rules expand the types of consulting services that impair auditor independence? What consulting services are not allowed under the Sarbanes-Oxley Act?

7. Under what circumstances may tax services be provided to public company audit clients? When might tax services impair auditor independence?

8. Who is responsible for certifying the financial statements filed with the SEC and how often will the certifications be made?

9. How recently must management's evaluation of internal control be to certify the financial statements filed with the SEC?

10. What are the two criteria that auditors consider when determining whether memos, correspondence, and other documents must be maintained in the audit files?

11. How long must auditors retain audit documentation?

12. Who is considered as "the client" when auditing public companies?

13. Which services must be pre-approved by the audit committee?

14. Which types of loans to executives are permitted by the Sarbanes-Oxley Act?

15. What is the auditor's reporting responsibility related to the client's internal controls?

16. Explain how the scope of internal controls tested by the auditor in an audit of the financial statements differs from controls tested by the auditor in an audit of internal controls.

17. What types of audit procedures does the auditor perform to provide a basis for the auditor's report on internal control?

18. Describe matters that the auditor must communicate to the audit committee of public companies.

19. What are the three conditions of fraud often referred to as "the fraud triangle?"

20. What sources are used by the auditor to gather information to assess fraud risks?

21. What are the three categories of auditor responses to fraud risks?

22. What procedures must the auditor perform to address the risk of management override of controls?

23. Will all CPA exam candidates take the same examination under the computer-based examination format? Explain.

24. Identify the four parts of the computer-based CPA exam. Identify the corresponding section on the paper-and-pencil exam for which transitional credit will be given.

MULTIPLE CHOICE QUESTIONS

1. Which of the following was *not* identified as an initial priority of the Public Company Accounting Oversight Board?
   a. A review of existing professional standards.
   b. Consideration of auditing standards required by the Sarbanes-Oxley Act.
   c. Consideration of exposure drafts issued by the ASB on audit risk.
   d. A review of standards for auditor attestation of internal controls as required by Section 404 of the Sarbanes-Oxley Act.

2. Which of the following is *not* a general principle used by the SEC in evaluating the effect of other services on auditor independence?
   a.   An auditor cannot function in the role of management.
   b.   The fee for the additional services must be less than the audit fee.
   c.   An auditor cannot audit his or her own work.
   d.   An auditor cannot serve in an advocacy role for the client.

3. In which of the following situations would an audit firm be considered not independent with respect to a public company audit client under the provisions of the Sarbanes-Oxley Act?
   a.   The client hires an audit firm member as its CFO. The CFO left the audit firm one month earlier, and participated in the most recent audit of the company.
   b.   The audit firm provides tax planning services to the client. The services were pre-approved by the audit committee.
   c.   The lead audit partner for the client has served in that capacity for the past four years.
   d.   The audit firm provides general business consulting services that were pre-approved by the audit committee.

4. Which of the following would prohibit management from being able to certify the annual financial statements?
   a.   The chief financial officer is not a CPA.
   b.   There are deficiencies, although not significant, in internal control
   c.   Management has not evaluated the effectiveness of its internal controls within the last six months.
   d.   Management has no knowledge of any untrue material facts contained in the financial statements.

5. Which of the following audit documents would *not* have to be retained in the audit files?
   a.   Working papers used to form the basis for the audit opinion.
   b.   Memos exchanged between audit team members that contain analyses of client financial data.
   c.   Emails summarizing conclusions about client business risks.
   d.   Superseded drafts of documents corrected for errors made by audit staff.

6. The SEC requires public companies to
   a.   Disclose waivers made to the code of ethics for senior management.
   b.   Have a code of ethics.
   c.   Include a "financial expert" on the audit committee.
   d.   Appoint a CPA as chair of the audit committee.

7. When providing an opinion on internal controls, the auditor
   a. Performs tests of a broader range of controls than those tested in the financial statement audit.
   b. Uses the understanding and testing of internal controls performed in the audit of the financial statements as the basis for the opinion on internal controls.
   c. Must only test controls when control risk is assessed below the maximum.
   d. Performs a combination of tests of controls and substantive procedures, including tests of details of balances.

8. Which of the following is an example of the "incentive/pressures" fraud condition?
   a. Selected financial statement ratios are not in compliance with covenants in bank loan documents.
   b. Material account balances are dependent on management estimation.
   c. Senior executives frequently waive internal control provisions.
   d. The majority of the board of directors consists of management.

PROBLEMS

1. The following situations involve the provision of non-audit services. Indicate whether providing the service is a violation of the requirements of the Sarbanes-Oxley Act and SEC rules.
   a. Providing bookkeeping services to a public company. The services were pre-approved by the audit committee of the company.
   b. Providing internal audit services to a public company that is not an audit client.
   c. Designing and implementing a financial information system for a private company.
   d. Recommending a tax shelter to a client that is publicly-held. The services were pre-approved by the audit committee.
   e. Providing internal audit services to a public company client with the pre-approval of the audit committee.
   f. Providing bookkeeping services to an audit client that is a private company.

2. During audit planning, the auditor obtained the following information:

   a. Management has a strong interest in employing inappropriate means to minimize reported earnings for tax-motivated reasons.

   b. Assets and revenues are based on significant estimates that involve subjective judgments and uncertainties that are hard to corroborate.

   c. The company is marginally able to meet exchange listing and debt covenant requirements.

   d. Significant operations are located and conducted across international borders in jurisdictions where differing business environments and cultures exist.

   e. There are recurring attempts by management to justify marginal or inappropriate accounting on the basis of materiality.

   f. The company's financial performance is threatened by a high degree of competition and market saturation.

Classify each of the six factors into one of these fraud conditions: incentives/pressures; opportunities; or attitudes/rationalization.

APPENDIX

SUMMARY OF KEY PROVISIONS OF THE
SARBANES-OXLEY ACT AFFECTING AUDITING AND
THE PUBLIC ACCOUNTING PROFESSION [1]

TITLE I – PUBLIC COMPANY ACCOUNTING OVERSIGHT BOARD

Section 101: Establishment; Administrative Provisions – The Public Company Oversight Board ("the Board") will have five financially-literate members, appointed for five-year terms. Two of the members must be or have been certified public accountants, and the remaining three must not be and cannot have been CPAs.

Section 102: Registration with the Board – Audit firms involved in the audits of public companies must register with the Board.

Section 103: Auditing, Quality Control, And Independence Standards And Rules – The Board will establish auditing and related attestation standards, quality control standards, and ethics standards to be used by registered accounting firms in the preparation and issuance of audit reports of issuers as required by the Act and SEC rules. The Board will include in auditing standards a requirement that registered accounting firms prepare and maintain workpapers for a period of at least seven years.

Section 104: Inspections of Registered Public Accounting Firms – Annual quality control inspections must be conducted every year for firms that audit more than 100 issuers. Other firms must be inspected at least once every 3 years. Special inspections may be requested by the SEC or Board.

Section 105: Investigations and Disciplinary Proceedings – If the Board determines that any registered firm has engaged in practices in violation of the Sarbanes-Oxley Act ("the Act"), the rules of the Board, or securities laws related to the issuance of audit reports, the Board may impose sanctions, including temporary suspension or permanent revocation of registration or association of individuals with a registered firm, monetary penalties, censure, additional education or training, or other sanctions provided by the rules of the Board.

---

[1] Only Titles and Sections of the Act that significantly affect auditing and the public accounting profession are included in this appendix. The full text of the Sarbanes-Oxley Act can be accessed through the AICPA website at *www.aicpa.org*.

TITLE II – AUDITOR INDEPENDENCE

Section 201: Services Outside the Scope Of Practice Of Auditors – It is unlawful for a registered public accounting firm to provide non-audit services to an issuer, including: (1) bookkeeping or other services related to the accounting records or financial statements of the audit client; (2) financial information systems design and implementation; (3) appraisal or valuation services, fairness opinions, or contribution-in-kind reports; (4) actuarial services; (5) internal audit outsourcing services; (6) management functions or human resources; (7) broker or dealer, investment adviser, or investment banking services; (8) legal services and expert services unrelated to the audit; (9) any other service that the Board determines, by regulation, is impermissible.

Other non-audit services may be provided if they are pre-approved by the audit committee. The audit committee will disclose to investors in periodic reports its decision to pre-approve non-audit services.

Section 203: Audit Partner Rotation – The lead audit or coordinating partner and the reviewing partner must rotate off the audit every 5 years.

Section 204: Auditor Reports to Audit Committees – The accounting firm must report to the audit committee all: 1) critical accounting policies and practices to be used; 2) all alternative treatments of financial information within GAAP that have been discussed with management, ramifications of the use of such alternative disclosures and treatments, and the treatment preferred by the accounting firm.

Section 206: Conflicts of Interest – The CEO, Controller, CFO, Chief Accounting Officer or person in an equivalent position cannot have been employed by the company's audit firm during the 1-year period preceding the audit.

Section 207: Study of Mandatory Rotation of Registered Public Accountants – The GAO will do a study on the potential effects of requiring the mandatory rotation of audit firms.

TITLE III – CORPORATE RESPONSIBILITY

Section 301: Public Company Audit Committees – Each member of the audit committee shall be an independent member of the board of directors of the issuer. The audit committee will be directly responsible for the appointment, compensation, and oversight of the work of any registered public accounting firm employed by the issuer.

Section 302: Corporate Responsibility For Financial Reports – The CEO and CFO of each issuer shall certify in each annual or quarterly report that: 1) they have reviewed the report; 2) based on their knowledge, the report does not contain any untrue statement or omit any material facts; 3) based on the their knowledge, the financial statements and disclosures fairly present in all material respects the operations and financial condition of the issuer; 4) that the officers are responsible for establishing and maintaining internal controls and have evaluated the effectiveness of internal controls; 5) they have disclosed to the auditors and audit committee all significant deficiencies in the design or operations of internal controls, and any fraud, whether or not material, that involves management or other employees with a significant role in the company's internal controls; and 6) any significant changes in internal controls subsequent to their evaluation of the controls.

Section 303: Improper Influence on Conduct of Audits – It shall be unlawful for any officer or director of an issuer to take any action to fraudulently influence, coerce, manipulate, or mislead any auditor engaged in the performance of an audit for the purpose of making the financial statements materially misleading.

TITLE IV – ENHANCED FINANCIAL DISCLOSURES

Section 404: Management Assessment Of Internal Controls – Requires the annual report of each issuer to include an internal control report which shall:

(1) state the responsibility of management for establishing and maintaining an adequate internal control structure and procedures for financial reporting; and

(2) contain an assessment, as of the end of the issuer's fiscal year, of the effectiveness of the internal control structure and procedures of the issuer for financial reporting.

The internal control report is to be attested to by the auditor as part of the audit engagement.

Section 407: Disclosure of Audit Committee Financial Expert –The SEC shall issue rules to require issuers to disclose whether at least one member of its audit committee is a financial expert as defined in Section 407 of the Act.

TITLE VII – STUDIES AND REPORTS

Section 701: GAO Study and Report Regarding Consolidation of Public Accounting Firms – The GAO will conduct a study to identify the factors that have led to the consolidation of accounting firms since 1989, the impact of the consolidation on capital formation and securities markets, and solutions to any problems identified, including ways to increase competition and the number of firms capable of providing audit services to large business organizations subject to the securities laws.

TITLE VIII – CORPORATE FRAUD AND CRIMINAL ACCOUNTABILITY ACT OF 2002

Section 802: Criminal Penalties for Altering Documents – It is a felony to knowingly destroy or create documents to impede, obstruct or influence any existing or contemplated federal investigation.

Section 806: Protection for Employees of Publicly Traded Companies who Provide Evidence of Fraud – Employees of issuers and accounting firms are extended whistleblower protection that would prohibit the employer from discharging or taking other action against employees who lawfully disclose information which the employee reasonably believes constitutes a violation of securities laws or Federal law relating to fraud against shareholders.

TITLE IX – WHITE-COLLAR CRIME PENALTY ENHANCEMENTS

Section 906: Failure of Corporate Officers to Certify Financial Reports – The CEO and CFO must certify that the financial statements and disclosures fully comply with provisions of the Securities Exchange Act and that they fairly present, in all material respects, the operations and financial condition of the issuer. Maximum penalties for willful certification of the financial statements knowing that they do not fully comply with the requirements are a fine of not more than $5,000,000 and/or imprisonment of up to 20 years.

TITLE XI – CORPORATE FRAUD AND ACCOUNTABILITY

Section 1102: Tampering With a Record or Otherwise Impeding an Official Proceeding – Any person who corruptly alters, destroys, mutilates, or conceals any record, document or other object with the intent to impair the object's integrity or availability for use in an official proceeding or to otherwise obstruct, influence or impede any official proceeding shall be fined and/or imprisoned for up to 20 years.